See that squirrel
in our tree?
I think he'd rather
live with me.

LAKESIDE

APARTMENTS

839

LAKESIDE APARTMENTS MANAGER APARTMENT 2

DELIVERIES IN REAR   USE LOBBY PHONE

dragonfly

fuchsia
plant

I'll wait awhile,
he could be shy.
Or maybe he likes it
way up high.

begonia plant

peanut

impatiens plant

ladybugs

Look!
Here he comes,
trying to hide.
He can't wait
to get inside.

He's in the flowers,
he's really bad.
He's digging up bulbs.
My mom is mad!

tulip bulb

American
Goldfinch

There he goes —
up the bricks
on his claws.
He steals seeds and
eats with his paws.

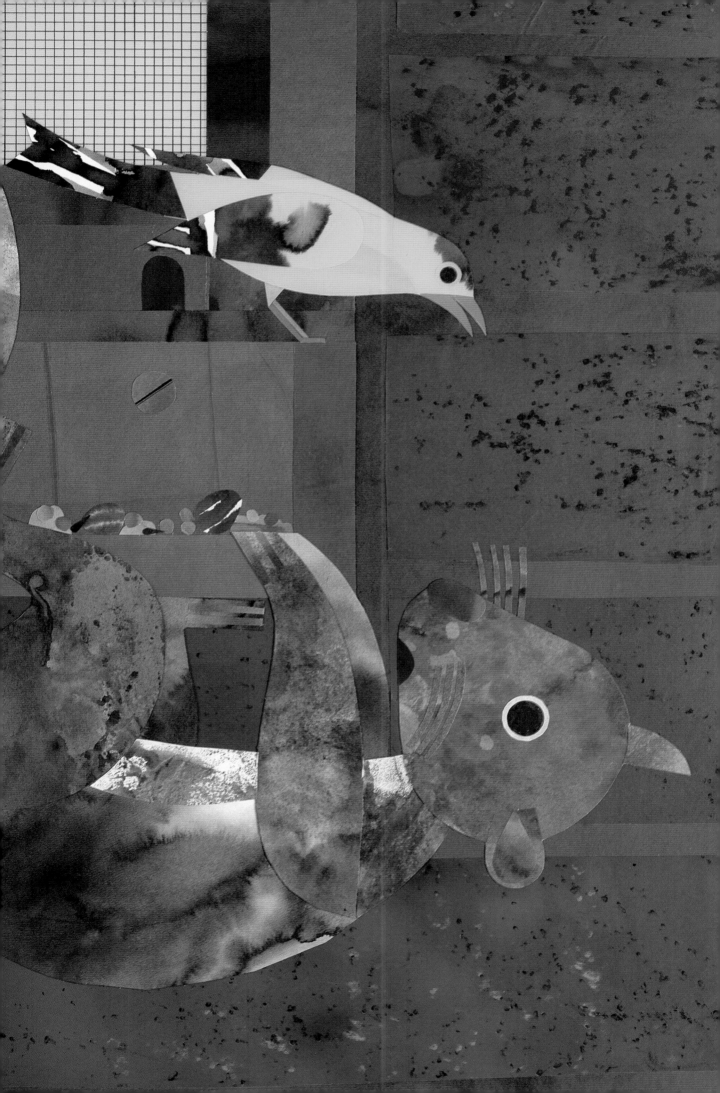

Walking
on tiptoe,
tail held high,
he brushes
my plants
as he zips by.

tomato
plant

monarch
butterfly

In our
window box,
watching us eat,
he sits on the flowers
and begs for a treat.

petunia
plants

I opened my window
for some fresh air,
but I forgot the screen
had a tear.

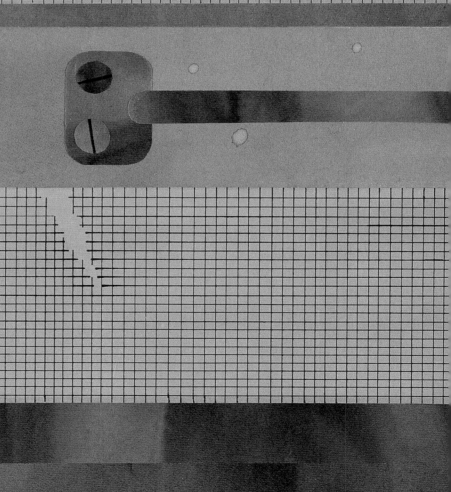

When I came back,
guess what I found?

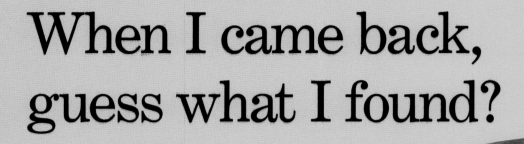

That squirrel was
there — looking around!

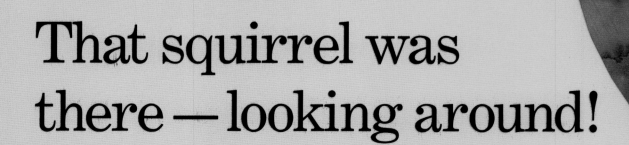

dandelion
plant

So I got some nuts,
ran out the door,
tapped one
on the sidewalk,
and left a few more.

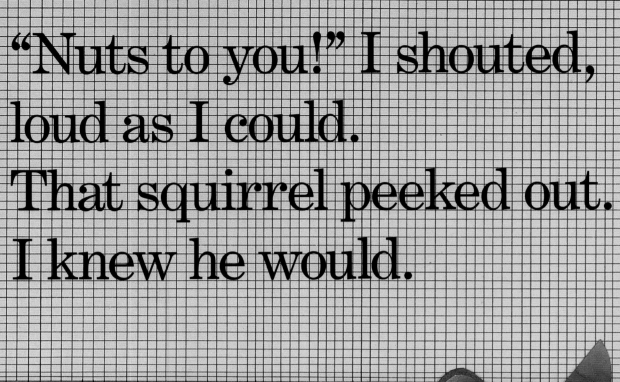

"Nuts to you!" I shouted,
loud as I could.
That squirrel peeked out.
I knew he would.

House Finch

He looked to the left.
He looked to the right.
He ran down the bricks
and took a big bite.

He ate all those nuts,
then scampered away,
but he'll get hungry
again someday.

I'll keep nuts
in my pockets,
one or two,
and when I see him,
I'll say:
"Nuts to you!"

garden hose

dusty
miller
plant

bumblebee

yellow jacket
wasp

coleus plants

Identification

Squirrels are classified as mammals, the group of animals that
nourish their young on milk from mammary glands, have hair
on their bodies, and have warm blood.

There are many different kinds of mammals, which are divided
into smaller groups. Squirrels are in a group called rodents, the
gnawing mammals. Squirrels live all over the world except for
Madagascar and Australia. They come in many different sizes —
some are as small as mice and some as large as cats. The squirrel
in this book is a gray squirrel whose head and body together
measure 8 to 10 inches, and whose tail measures 7¾ to 10 inches.

Teeth

Squirrels, like all rodents, have gnawing teeth. Gray squirrels have two incisors on the top and two on the bottom of their jaws. These teeth are big and strong and, as they are constantly being worn down with use, continue growing throughout the squirrel's life. Squirrels also have smaller teeth at the sides of their mouth.

Feet

Most squirrels have four toes on their front feet and five on their hind feet. Their claws are very sharp, so they can climb trees (and brick walls, too).

honeybee

flies

Tail

The tail is covered with fur, can be very bushy, and is about as long as the squirrel's body. A squirrel uses its tail for many things: it's an umbrella in rain or hot sun, a blanket in winter, and a rudder when swimming. It also acts as a furry balancing rod when the squirrel is climbing or leaping from branch to branch.

Nest/Home

Gray squirrels are tree squirrels. They love trees, though you often see them on the ground. They live in holes in trees or in big leaf nests they build in high branches or in the forks of trees. You can see their nests most easily in winter, when the tree branches are bare.

calla lily
plants

Food

Gray squirrels like to eat nuts, including acorns, hickory nuts, walnuts, beechnuts, and pecans. They also eat maple seeds, corn, pine seeds, and fruit. If you want to feed squirrels, leave nuts for them on the ground. Don't ever let them take a nut from your hand. Remember that squirrels are wild animals and can bite or scratch.

You may have watched a squirrel dig a hole with its front feet and then bury a nut, maybe one you put out. Then the squirrel covers it up by patting the dirt with its feet and nose. It's laying in a food supply for winter. Did you ever wonder how squirrels remember where they bury all those nuts? Squirrels have sensitive noses and can smell food even under the snow. They forget some, though, and those nuts sprout into many, many trees.

Artist Lois Ehlert loves watching squirrels from the windows of her studio while she works. She is the creator of many award-winning books for children, including *In My World; Growing Vegetable Soup; Planting a Rainbow; Red Leaf, Yellow Leaf;* the best-selling *Waiting for Wings;* and, most recently, *Pie in the Sky.*

Nuts to You! was inspired by an actual experience she had with one of the squirrels in her Milwaukee neighborhood.